FEARLESS & FABULOUS

10 POWERFUL STRATEGIES
FOR GETTING ANYTHING YOU WANT IN LIFE

CARA ALWILL LEYBA

Passionista PUBLISHING

FEARLESS & FABULOUS

Cover art © Cara Loper/Loose Lid Creative
www.looselidcreative.com

Interior design by Ryan Leyba

ISBN-13: 978-0692252963

Passionista
PUBLISHING

For every woman who has a dream of living a better life.
And for my mother, who taught me I deserve nothing less.

CONTENTS

FOREWARD

by Jonna Spilbor

From the moment I had enough hair on my head to squeeze a couple of curly tufts into pigtails, I knew my career would find me in front of a camera.

Since I had formulated that thought at a time when my age and my shoe size were equally miniscule, I was blissfully unaware that there were several different career opportunities within the entertainment industry. So, I fixated on becoming a movie star as my way in.

In fact, one of the very first real conversations I remember having with my mother happened before I hit kindergarten, and it went something like this: "Mom, how come you're not an actress?"

She replied, "Well honey, not everyone in the world wants to be an actress."

I can't remember exactly what came out of my four-year-old mouth at the time, but I can articulate today that my mother may as well have been speaking monster. In my young, endearingly unruly brain, I simply could not fathom how any person on the planet wouldn't want to be famous! To this day, a teeny tiny part of me still clings tight to that four-year-old's wistful confusion.

Fast forward a few decades, and I'm happy to say I'm not only living *that* dream, but I have learned how to harness the fearlessness that came so easily as a child to bring my grown-up goals to life. Teach yourself to dream without limits, and you will achieve without limits.

I think back so very fondly to those yesterdays. Days when daydreaming was as big a part of our routine as breathing and blinking. Days when all we needed to become a full-blown superhero was a cape and two outstretched arms. Days when we unwittingly fed our little brains big, lofty goals and never, not for a second, doubted we could achieve them. Days when sandbox sand became a new and exciting city until we were summoned inside for dinner. When a rope and a tire allowed us to fly. When we befriended bugs and caught them in a jar, never once contemplating the cruelty of mortality – theirs or ours.

Have you ever wondered why those truly were "'the days'"?

I will tell you why. You see, children are fearless.

A child's mind is fertile, limitless and expansive. Physically, a child will naturally outgrow her high chair, her baby shoes and her big wheel, but she never outgrows her dreams. Never, ever. So why, then, do so many of us grow into the adults we are today, but have yet to fulfill our highest goals and aspirations?

If you have ever stayed in a job you hate, or lingered in a crappy relationship, or wouldn't know a personal boundary if it bit you on the butt, then this book is about to change your life.

There is one thing, and only one thing, holding us back from creating the life of our dreams.

Fear.

It's not money. It's not education. It's not our looks, our relationships, or our responsibilities that keep us from going out and getting everything we want. All of these things are merely excuses. We create these roadblocks in our own heads, as if they were hope traps ("There goes another hope! Better not let it loose or I actually may fulfill a goal!"). Self-imposed hope traps are the way in which we keep our dreams under wraps, and hold ourselves back from forging ahead into the life we long to lead.

I'll say it again. The one thing that holds us back from creating the life of our dreams, is fear. That's it. That's all. Eliminate fear, and there is nothing you can't do!

"Oh, is that *all?*" you ask. "Simple as that, huh? Just forget my fear, and poof! Like magic here comes my dream job, my dream relationship and my dream bank account? Sounds like the only one dreaming here is *you!*"

Okay then, humor me.

You have before you one of the greatest tools to get you started on your new, fearless path. Read it cover to cover. Put the techniques to good use, and choose one thing in your present circumstance you would like to change. Just one. Then ask yourself, "How would I behave in this circumstance *if I had no fear?*"

Got it? Now close your eyes, and see yourself as the five-year-old superhero you once were. See yourself as the six-year-old kicking her legs to the sky on a tree swing. See yourself as the little girl who built cities in sandboxes and befriended bugs in a jar.

Feels familiar, doesn't it? It should. Because she is you... *without fear.*

Your fabulously "Fearless" life starts right now.

Enjoy each moment of your new and exciting journey, and if ever you're in doubt, please repeat after me.

Just be fearless.

With much love to the author, and to my sexy sisters everywhere,

Jonna Spilbor
Attorney, Radio Host, Author, Motivational Speaker and TV Legal Analyst/Contributor

INTRODUCTION
WHAT WOULD YOU DO IF YOU WEREN'T AFRAID?

"Everything you want is on the other side of fear."
— *Jack Canfield*

Chances are if you've picked up this book, there are things you want to do in your life but up until this point, you've been too scared to do them. Maybe you've filed them away onto your "bucket list" or maybe you've just become content with that fact that you'll never even attempt them because for some reason, fear tells you that you shouldn't. Perhaps it's fear of failure, or fear of rejection. Maybe it's fear of being judged, or not liked. Or perhaps it's even fear of your own success or personal happiness (how's *that* for jumpin' right in?).

Fear can be responsible for changing your life – for better or for worse. If fear persists, you run the risk of missing out on some of the greatest experiences life has to offer. If you can overcome your fears, you open yourself up to a world beyond your wildest imagination. I wrote this book because I believe everyone deserves to live a remarkable life. With loving support and guidance, we all have the power to be extraordinary.

Now let's get something straight before we go any further. We all have fears. True "fearlessness" does not really exist. When I refer to being fearless, I'm talking about recognizing that you have fears, but deciding to move forward anyway. That's a biggie.

A fearless and fabulous woman is someone who recognizes her desires, has the confidence to chase her dreams, and believes that everything is possible. She does not believe in the word "failure." She redefines it. To the fearless and fabulous woman, a "failure" is just a signal that she needs to change her course and try a new way of doing something. She thinks positively, takes consistent action toward her goals, and never gives up.

Nothing makes me sadder than seeing a woman with boundless talent and aspirations who has let fear take the wheel. There are far too many people out there who are stifling their own success because they are afraid to make the first move. Can you imagine what an amazing world this would be if we all fearlessly stepped into our full potential?

It may seem daunting to look at your dreams and truly believe that you have the power to make all of them a reality. It takes a lot of work and even more faith to move past fear and make things happen, but it's *far* from impossible. I genuinely believe that every single woman has the capability to conquer her fears and live the life of her dreams. Why am I so confident? Because I've done it myself, in fact I'm still doing it, and I've helped countless other women do it as well. As a Certified Master Life Coach and self-proclaimed Inspirationista, I have taught workshops, coached women all around the world, and spent years researching this very topic. I have helped hundreds of women harness their vision and create serious shifts in their lives. I have seen it happen first-hand, and let me tell you, it's pretty damn awesome. As a result, I have developed a foolproof way to live a fearless and fabulous life. And guess what? It's really not that hard.

How This Book Works

This book will teach you ten powerful strategies that will help you overcome your fears and live the fabulous life you're meant to live. And we're gonna get real – fast. I purposely kept this book short because I'm all about action. If you've read my other books, you know I don't dance around topics. My job is to get you thinking in a fresh, focused mindset and inspire you to start making things happen, glass of champagne in hand.

Each chapter outlines one strategy and includes short exercises so that you can start putting these strategies in motion immediately. I urge you to read through this book with an open-mind. Tuck your doubts away and be fully present during each assignment so that you get the most out of this experience. You should have a journal next to you as you go through each chapter (preferably a really fabulous one!) so that you can take notes and complete the exercises. There are also areas to write directly in this book if you're reading the paperback version.

At the end of each chapter, look for the *Fearless & Fabulous* logo. I've included a manifesto that sums up that chapter. These are great little reminders that you can highlight and come back to whenever you need a boost.

I've also included success stories from women I have either worked with personally or been inspired by to illustrate some of these strategies. These women are the epitome of fearless and fabulous! Dig into their stories and get inspired. They are the real deal.

This book is here for you to reference as often as you need. Keep it loaded on your Kindle, or keep a copy stashed in your purse at all times. It's meant for you to whip out whenever you need a boost, so feel free to mark it up with a hot pink high-lighter, fold over pages that stand out for you, and share it with your girlfriends. Think of it as your fearless and fabulous Bible.

Are you getting excited? Nervous? Good! This book is meant to shake you up and turn you on. You're gonna to have to be very honest with yourself, and work really, really hard. But in the end, you'll be so grateful that you did. So put your worries aside and dust off those dreams, sister. You are about to become fearless and fabulous!

ONE

DECIDE WHAT YOU WANT

"Follow your bliss and the universe will open doors for you
where there were only walls."
— *Joseph Campbell*

I want you to answer this question: what do you want? What
are your deepest desires? What do you require as a human being
to ensure that you live your best life? And for the record, living
your best life is exactly what you deserve. In order to answer this
question in the most honest way, you have to put everyone else's
opinions and needs aside. I'm not asking you what you *think* you
should want. I'm not asking you what your parents think you
should want. In a perfect world, what do *you* desire?

I've watched so many women trapped in a state of fear because they were striving for a dream that wasn't their own. Let's
imagine that you are trying to buy a home. You're saving every
penny and applying for a mortgage, but you're petrified. Let's
also imagine that you're trying to buy this home because you
were raised to believe that you should own a piece of real estate

as an adult. In your heart, you know you aren't ready to make that kind of commitment. You still want to travel, you don't have enough money in the bank to comfortably make a down payment, and your job is unstable. And if we're honest, there are *far* too many pairs of Jimmy Choos yet to be purchased. Yet you're still trying moving forward while paralyzed with fear because you think buying this home is what you should do.

Now let's imagine that you're planning a trip around the world. It's always been your dream to travel. You don't like to fly, and you're still trying to save enough money to be able to afford the plane tickets, but you are thrilled at the thought of taking this trip. You have a burning desire to see the world, and you'll make it happen come hell or high water. Sure, you're scared shitless, *but your passion outweighs your fear.*

Do you see the difference?

It's so much easier to move through fear when we truly desire what's on the other side of it. The trick is channeling that passion and focusing on the parts you're excited about as opposed to the parts that terrify you. When you can achieve that mindset, everything is possible.

My decision to publish my first book, *Sparkle: The Girl's Guide to Living a Deliciously Dazzling, Wildly Effervescent, Kick-Ass Life,* was laced with fear. I had been signed to one of New York's top literary agents and we had shopped the book (which initially had a different title) to major publishers, only to be rejected by every single one of them. Nineteen, to be exact. All came back with a similar response: "It's not the right fit for us." There were many reasons: some had just taken on a similar book, some did not feel the topic was aligned with their expertise, and others just simply weren't interested. I was crushed, but I was not giving up. Most authors would have crawled in a hole and surrendered their dream by that point. But that wasn't going to be my story. My book may not have been the right fit for those publishers, but it was the right fit for my readers, and that's why I knew I was going to publish it – someway, somehow. By that point, I was ready to sky-write the damn thing.

I had to make a major decision: rewrite the book and stick with my agent in the hopes that we could re-pitch it, or believe in my project and self-publish. I was scared to put my work out into the world and become vulnerable to the harsh critical eye of the public, especially without a major publisher behind me. Yet my burning desire to get my work out there is what drove me through my fear. I had dreamed of writing a book since the second grade. I always wanted to be a published author, and I believed I deserved to be, even if I didn't have the support I thought I needed. Though I was scared, the thought of not achieving that dream became *even scarier* for me.

I challenged my inner fearless and fabulous self and chose to move forward with self-publishing despite my fears. I knew it would be a daunting task (with lots of blood, sweat, and Pinot Noir involved), but I maintained a positive mindset and developed a strategy to stay focused on the excitement of the project. I had absolutely no experience with self-publishing, so I had to do my homework. I researched until my eyes bled and then researched some more. I hired an editor, worked tirelessly with my designer on the cover, and basically lived online gathering as much information as I could to ensure this book was done right.

Every day, I woke up and committed to my passion in some form or another. Whether it was writing a certain amount of words, or approving cover designs, or engaging my future readers through social media, I spent my energy propelling my dream into reality rather than getting caught up in my own my anxiety. I channeled that fearless woman I knew lived deep within me (if you need a visual, she prances around in five-inch Louboutins and has really toned arms) and she is one *fabulous bitch*. Whenever I found myself paralyzed with fear, I pictured her crushing that fear with her spiked heels and a steaming hot soy latte in hand and I quickly got over it. You can spend your energy getting excited or being afraid. The choice is yours.

Sparkle went on to become a #1 Amazon bestseller in multiple categories, multiple times. It received rave reviews from readers all around the world, and it continues to sell tons of copies. I've received heartfelt emails from readers that have literally brought me to tears. I've met readers and signed copies of my book in New York, London and Paris. How bad-ass is that? If I had let my fear consume me, I would have never had those life-changing experiences. And I would have never gone on to produce more books like this one.

FEARLESS & FABULOUS EXERCISE

It's time to whip out that ultra-fab journal and grab your pink pen to declare your desires. Then, write down all the reasons why you want those things. Get as detailed as possible. Remember: the details and the "whys" are what get us excited.

_____

_____

_____

_____

_____

_____

_____

Your Life is Your Own. Act Accordingly.

Did you know that the #1 regret of the dying is that they did not live a life that was true to themselves? A palliative nurse did a study on the most common regrets of the dying and published her results in a book titled *The Top Five Regrets of the Dying*. The top regret was that they lived a life that others expected of them. "This was the most common regret of all. When people realize that their life is almost over and look back clearly on it, it is easy to see how many dreams have gone unfulfilled. Most people had not honored even half of their dreams and had to die knowing that it was due to choices they had made, or not made. Health brings a freedom very few realize, until they no longer have it."

Can you imagine being on your deathbed with an aching feeling that you did not live your life to the fullest? I don't know about you, but that thought terrifies me and is enough to push me forward through my fears. Life is too short to be stuck with the "would haves" "could haves" and "should haves." It's on you to make sure you live every second as if it was your last. Life is precious and not guaranteed, and that is something I remind myself of every single day. When fear strikes I ask myself: Will I regret not doing this when I'm eighty years old? If the answer is yes, I step into action. Plus, don't you want great stories to talk about over a glass of champagne when you're in the nursing home?

FEARLESS
&FABULOUS

You can spend your energy getting excited or being afraid.
The choice is yours.

TWO

OWN YOUR DESIRES

"The more you love your decisions, the less you
need others to love them."
— *Unknown*

Many of us are nurturers at heart. Whether we are a mother,
sister, wife, or best friend, we as women tend to be really good
at caring for those around us. And while that is a fantastic char-
acteristic to possess, it's crucial that we put our own needs first.
This does not make us selfish, it makes us fulfilled and happy
– two key qualities to living a fearless and fabulous life. If your
own needs are not met, you will never be able to bust through
the blocks that hold you back and ultimately keep you in a place
of fear and desolation. This is one of the most single important
takeaways from this book, so bust out that hot pink marker and
highlight that last sentence, ladies!

It can be difficult to own your desires, especially when you
love to see those around you happy. I've worked with dozens
of women who are holding back their greatness because they're

so worried about letting someone down in their life. Perhaps you're thinking about changing careers, but your parents put you through school to get an MBA so that you can earn that six-figure salary in finance. They rave about you to all of their friends, but deep down you're completely miserable in your job. Maybe you have a burning desire to quit that job in finance and teach yoga full-time, but the thought of even expressing that desire to your parents scares you to death. You know they will be disappointed in you, so you remain in your stressful, unfulfilling job day in and day out just to keep other people happy. Do you realize how unfair that is? Not only are you depriving yourself of a bliss-filled, passionate life, you're actually depriving your parents of a bliss-filled, passionate child. You may not even realize it, but you are forever changed as a person when you remain chained to a life that is not aligned with your authentic self. Little by little, you begin to lack the exuberance, creativity, and the appetite for life that you once had. *And it shows.*

Here's something important to remember: people will get over it. As long as you are treating those around you with kindness and respect, nothing else should matter. Your personal choices and decisions on how you decide to live your life are just that: personal. The things that make you happy are priceless and the people who love you should understand that completely. And if they don't, it's not your problem.

FEARLESS & FABULOUS SUCCESS STORY
An Essay by Debbie Vasquez, Project Manager

Years ago, my life was in disarray. I was divorced, my ex had an accident that caused brain damage and could no longer function in the work place, leaving me to deal with a devastated child and being fully responsible for our daughter. I was working at one of the three major local companies and met a small business owner who offered me employment at his company. The opportunity would be to work from home as the company was not in my local area.

Family and friends, especially my parents, were not supportive of this opportunity. They felt the stability of this unknown company was risky – and what about insurance? Despite the risks of taking the job, what I did know is that I needed to be home for my daughter more than ever because her father was no longer in her life the way he had been. I did not want my daughter growing up remembering that neither of us was around.

I was paralyzed by indecision for nine months. It was difficult enough my parents did not agree with my decision to get divorced, but the fact that they thought I was making the wrong career decision just felt like a heavy burden to bear.

Only one person in my life actually encouraged me to make that move and it is my now husband. It was not because he totally understood or agreed, but he knew I was not happy and this change would give me an opportunity to focus on what I felt was the most important aspect of my life – my daughter. While others, including my parents, questioned the company and the career opportunities, they never asked me if I was happy. Was I comfortable? Yes. I knew the company, I knew my job, I knew what would happen every day and I knew I had a paycheck. Did I know that this new opportunity would be better? No! I was so scared but being at home when my daughter came home from school every day beat any career opportunity that I could miss.

After agnozing over the decision, I took the job, and it was the best decision I ever made. Looking back, I do believe friends and family thought they were looking out for me but most just didn't understand that a traditional job was not working for me. I had to pursue an opportunity to have the life I had always wanted even if it meant I was going against the grain and against the type of life my parents led, the type of life they expected me to have.

Ultimately, however, it was not about 'my' career – it was about being a mother and being there for my daughter. Any decision has pros and cons and what I have learned is that you need to focus on the pros so that the cons do not drag you down.

Within four years, my company went through restructuring and I was asked to be part of the beginning of those changes. I had no idea how many hours I would end up putting into the company, but I was always there for my daughter because I was home. I can still hear the bus stop in front of my house, and I remember the sound of her foot-steps (or foot stomping depending on the day!) and mostly, I was able to be the parent that I could not have been in an office. She grew up in the times of chat rooms and the beginnings of instant messaging. I believe she had the potential to be vulnerable to these new technolo-gies but I was physically there to prevent her from 'meeting' people she did not know. I think too many parents want to be friends and I was, and still am, a parent. I parent first. It's my role. I'm very, very proud of the woman my daughter has become and I'm proud of the company that I continue to work for – which also hired my husband and brother! Life is good ... not perfect, but I don't believe perfect ex-ists. If it did – what would we have to strive for?

Debbie's decision to trust her gut was clearly a great one. Only she knew what was best for her and her family, and by tak-ing that leap despite the negativity or doubt from those around her, she designed a life that she loves. As she states, nothing is perfect, but she has taken ownership for her choices and she's pretty damn proud of them. Debbie should be an inspiration for all of us!

Surround Yourself with The Best

Oprah Winfrey once said, "Surround yourself with only those who will lift you higher." That powerful advice could not be truer. As you step into the fearless and fabulous version of yourself, you will undoubtedly meet people who are not supportive. If you've experienced a negative response any time you've made a decision that required you to move ahead in the face of fear, understand that the cause of the negativity most likely has nothing to do with you at all. For instance, in Debbie's situation, she experienced uncertainty and doubt from those around her. Their fears did not exist because they lacked faith in Debbie, they existed because of the stories they had heard or things they believed. The fear belonged to *them*, based on *their own* experiences.

Whenever we make a powerful choice for ourselves, for instance the decision to leave a job, it forces others around us to look at their own lives and choices. Your decision to grow may reflect their decision to stagnate. I call it the mirror effect. But that's ultimately not your concern. You can only hope to inspire someone with your fabulosity; nothing else is required of you aside from rocking out as your true, authentic self.

So what's a gal to do when everyone around her seems like a Negative Nelly? Simple! Change your surroundings, stat. Seek support from mentors, colleagues, support groups, or friends and family members who can relate to what you're going through. I have found some of the greatest support from both online and in-person networking groups. Sharing my thoughts and fears with women who share some of those same feelings has been invaluable in my journey. When you can be open and honest with someone who will not judge your decisions, you're able to be open and honest with yourself. Create a network that will help lift you up, encourage you, and challenge you to be as amazing as you know you can be.

FEARLESS & FABULOUS EXERCISE

What are you holding back doing because you're worried about someone else's opinion? Write it down here or in your journal. Getting it down on paper will help propel you forward.

_____

_____

_____

_____

_____

_____

_____

Everything is a Choice

How many times have you caught yourself saying, "I wish I could do X but I just can't." Sure there are some things in life that are physically impossible (unfortunately, I can't snap my fingers and time travel back into 1986 to attend a Wham concert), but for the most part, everything is a choice. Let's take for example changing careers, as this is a big dream for so many women. You may have said to yourself at some point, "I'd love to leave my job, but I can't because I'm tied to this mortgage and car payments." Let's get something straight, ladies. You are not forced to stay in a job you hate and you are not forced to pay a mortgage or car payments. You are not a victim of anything in this life. You choose to get up and go to work every day, and you choose to pay your mortgage and your car payments. When you frame it like that, you immediately reclaim the control and take yourself out of what I like to call "victim mode." Fearless and fabulous women are not victims. Tattoo that on your forehead if you have to, because it's a theme we're going to remind ourselves of constantly as we go through this book. Got it?

Because you are a responsible adult, you probably wouldn't just quit your job without a backup plan and stop paying your mortgage or car payments, but you can develop a plan to change all of those things if you really want to. You own the decision to get up and go to work every day. And you can own the decision to look for a new job just as easily. And you know what? If you choose to quit without a backup plan, that's your choice too.

Recognizing that everything is a choice gives us a sense of power and control. This can be comforting if you experience fear and anxiety. It's scary to feel like life is happening *to you*. There is nothing worse than feeling like things are spinning out of control and you can't do anything to change it. But that is never true. Can we control everything that happens? Absolutely not. But what we can control is the way we respond to those things. Start viewing every single part of your life as a choice, and then decide what you need to boldly and fearlessly change.

I realize I've been talking about some pretty big life changes so far. But the most important thing to remember is that being fearless and fabulous does not mean you need a complete life or career overhaul. Rather than imagining changing your entire life around in order to face your fears (hello, anxiety!), try adding the things you've always wanted to do into your life, little by little. For example, let's say you want to switch careers and become a writer. That's obviously a big step that needs a lot of planning, but you can start small. Try writing a little bit each night. Start that book you've always dreamed of publishing by jotting down an outline. Incorporate your passion into your life however you can and I promise you'll instantly feel better.

FEARLESS
&FABULOUS

You are forever changed as a person when you remain chained to a life that is not aligned with your authentic self.

THREE

GET CONFIDENT

"Believe in yourself and there will come a day when others have
no choice but to believe in you."
— *Cynthia Kersey*

Negative thought patterns and self-limiting beliefs are surefire confidence killers that can keep us locked into our fears.
Fearless and fabulous have one very important thing in common:
they think positively and radiate confidence. In this chapter, I'm
going to help you drop those pesky insecurities and challenge
your negative thinking so that you can rewire your brain (yes, it's
possible!).

Many of us have self-limiting beliefs. Sometimes we don't
even realize they are there. Maybe yours look something like
this: "I really want to lose weight but I've always been heavy. I'm
just not the type to be thin." Or, "I want to be a full-time writer,
but I'll never make money doing that." It's important to understand that these beliefs are not real; they are fear-based.

So where do they come from? Self-limiting beliefs can come

from oh-so-many places. Often times, we learn certain things as children and we never question them. For example, your parents may have taught you that in order to live a happy, successful life, you should go to college, get a good job, get married and have children. You may not want to follow that path, but you feel you'll never have a happy, successful life any other way. If you really break it down, does that make sense? Or are you just taking their word for it? Dig deep to the root of those beliefs and determine whether or not they are actually true.

FEARLESS & FABULOUS EXERCISE

Identify your self-limiting beliefs and negative thought patterns. Keep a journal throughout the day and write them down when they surface, or list them here.

_____

_____

_____

_____

_____

_____

_____

Once you become aware of these beliefs, the next step is to challenge them. *This* is where the magic happens. Our minds are powerful beyond measure, so just as quickly as those thoughts appear, you can train your brain to defy them. Ask yourself the following questions: Is this belief true? Where did this thought originate? Is there evidence to support this? If so, what are some examples?

This process gets you thinking deeply about these beliefs and most often you will find that there is no evidence to support them at all.

FEARLESS & FABULOUS EXERCISE

Refer back to the list you just made. For every self-limiting belief you wrote, I want you to now write down where you believe that thought originated.

Example:

Self-limiting belief: I am too old to switch careers.

Where it originated: My parents told me that I should choose my career by the age of 25 and I am now 37.

_____

_____

_____

_____

_____

_____

_____

_____

Look at your list. Are those things truth? Or have you just believed them because someone told you that you should? Spend a few minutes on this one and let it sink in.

Now it's time to challenge these beliefs. The best way to do this is to find examples from your past to prove these beliefs wrong. For example, let's say you're trying to save money for a big move across the country. Your self-limiting beliefs may tell you that you'll never be able to pull it off, it's too big of a goal, and you're just not that disciplined. Where did that thought come from? Maybe it's what society has taught you. Maybe you've grown up believing you should put your roots down in one place and settle down. You've identified it, now it's time to challenge it.

I'd encourage you to take a look back at your life and think about a time where you *were* disciplined. Maybe it was your last semester in college where you got through your finals and graduated with honors. Or maybe that time you lost twenty-five pounds. Chances are, you've been able to pull off some pretty major things in the past, so use those accomplishments to give you the confidence fuel your new goals. You are much more powerful than you give yourself credit.

And believe me, I get it. It's not easy to challenge and overcome these nasty little lingering beliefs, but it is completely possible. It's just going to take self-awareness and hard work. You're going to have to make this a daily habit that you practice religiously. Keep your journal with you and commit to being aware of your thoughts all day long. Like I said, our minds are extremely powerful so it's up to you to rewrite your story, but it will take patience and persistence.

Just as you can convince yourself that you are lacking, you can also convince yourself that you are abundant. As Henry Ford said, "Whether you think you can, or you think you can't, either way you are right." Start replacing your negative, self-limiting beliefs with powerful, positive beliefs. Your gifts and talents are unlimited; you just have to tap into the confidence to believe it.

Celebrate Your Strengths

I know how easy it is to focus on your weakness, but you're going to have to learn to celebrate your strengths in order to become a fearless and fabulous woman. This practice helps you develop a healthy self-esteem and helps you move into a more positive state of mind. Honing in on what you love about yourself is the quickest way to kick negativity to the curb (while wearing your favorite stilettos, of course). As important as this exercise is, it can be challenging. Many of us feel uncomfortable celebrating ourselves because we feel that it's narcissistic, but that could not be farther from the truth. If you don't celebrate yourself, who will?

In order to channel a sense of confidence, think about the way you'd talk to a child. Would you identify that child's weaknesses and focus solely on what they need to improve upon? Of course not! You'd nurture that child by showcasing their strengths in a positive light and using those strengths to help them breed even more confidence. You'd tell them what they are great at and highlight examples of their success. It's time to start doing the same thing for yourself.

FEARLESS & FABULOUS EXERCISE
Write down five of your strengths you can celebrate!

_____

_____

_____

_____

_____

How have those strengths helped you in the past?

_____

_____

_____

_____

_____

Smarten Up

One of the biggest causes for insecurity is lack of knowledge. And I totally get it. You can't rock true confidence if you feel like you have nothing to back it up. Imagine you're running for mayor of a town you've never lived in. Imagine that not only are you unfamiliar with that town, but you know absolutely nothing about politics. Even if you channeled your best "fake it till you make it" attitude, your confidence would probably be quickly slashed if you were forced to speak to a crowd of people in a town hall meeting. It's virtually impossible to be confident if we are not knowledgeable.

So how can you gain confidence? Smarten up! If you're insecure about your career, take courses and educate yourself on your industry. Look toward people in your community that you can learn from. Get a mentor. You will immediately feel better when you learn new information and share it with others. Knowledge is power. And power builds confidence.

Develop Your Confidence From Within

When I was in my early 20s, my confidence was on a serious roller coaster ride at all times. If I was in a relationship and things were going well with that guy, I was on a self-esteem high. If I landed a new job, I felt on top of the world. Yet, on the opposite end of the spectrum, if said guy broke up with me, I was crushed. My confidence was zapped and I felt like the lowest of the low. If I didn't get the call back from a job I wanted, I felt worthless.

Yet something interesting happened when I entered my thirties. Suddenly my confidence remained balanced despite what was going on in my life. I credit this to a resolute belief that I was good enough no matter what. I began to understand through experience that life was a series of ups and downs, and I was no better or worse a person because of what was going on around me. I was a little older, a little wiser, and a lot happier. Things were always in flux, and as long as I could focus on what I loved about myself, I could get through anything.

As you embark on your fearless and fabulous journey, pay close attention to how you feel about yourself. Identify the triggers that challenge your self-worth. If a relationship ends and you feel like you'll never meet someone else, flip the script. View it as an opportunity to discover yourself again. Capitalize on that precious alone time and do things that make you happy. If you lose your job, view that as a chance to discover what really lights you up. You get the picture. Once you realize that you can control the way you feel no matter what is going on around you, a sense of confidence will take center stage and your fears will begin to fade away.

FEARLESS & FABULOUS SUCCESS STORY
An Essay by Annette Callan

Most people who know me would probably describe me as asser-tive, but what they don't know is that being assertive is extremely difficult for me. I have all kinds of reasons why it's so hard for me to say what's on my mind, confront a difficult situation, or stand up for myself.. For me, it came down to fear of someone not liking me, not feeling worthy, and the fear of looking like an idiot.

Not long ago, my manager was let go and I began reporting to his boss, the Director. She is smart, experienced, and educated. My inner thoughts spun with self-doubt and negative talk while I listened to her speak on company calls. I wondered if I was good enough to work for her. I questioned myself, doubted my work and began to get really nervous when I had to update her on a project. The time came when I needed to work with her on a daily basis and I knew I needed to be confident in my recommendations. I wanted to impress her. I needed to be more assertive, not only for my career but for my self-worth. I had to force myself to see this as an opportunity. An opportunity to be proud of the work I do, proud of my foresight in my projects and proud of the relationships I build! I planned our meetings to be extremely produc-tive. I spent each evening preparing for the next day, the next meeting and the one after that. It worked! She was pleased with my work. She respected my opinions, asked for my recommendations and praised me! All the negative thoughts in my head were gone...for that moment.

Even now, I let doubt creep in, I'm human...but I use the energy to prepare. I give myself the time to be the best I can be and know that I have the knowledge and wisdom to succeed!

Annette's story is a perfect example of how you can use your fearful energy to fuel your success. She learned how to manage her fear and spend her time and energy focusing on how she could win the respect of her boss. Annette became present to her fear, yet walked through it anyway by focusing on what she was good at doing. She celebrated her strengths rather than wallowing in her self-doubt. And as she admits, her fears have not completely disappeared, but she has learned how to move ahead regardless. Go Annette!

FEARLESS
*&***FABULOUS**

Genuine confidence comes from within. Celebrate what you love about yourself and give up your self-limiting beliefs.

FOUR

GET UNCOMFORTABLE

"Life begins at the end of your comfort zone."
— *Neale Donald Walsch*

One of the biggest reasons people hesitate to leap fearlessly into their dreams is because they assume they have to do it all at once. There is nothing more frightening than stepping into the unknown, especially when you're not yet fully comfortable experiencing fear. But in order to be fearless and fabulous, you're going to have to learn to get uncomfortable.

Life is easy when we're in our comfort zone. It's effortless and cozy to remain stagnant and just go through the motions of everyday life. There's a sense of dependability that we as humans need in order to feel safe and secure. From a scientific standpoint, your comfort zone is a behavioral state of routine and patterns that provides low anxiety, regular happiness, and limited stress. Doesn't sound so bad, huh? *Not so fast!* If you want to stretch out into your full potential and truly live an extraordinary life, you're going to have to get out of that cocoon. Nothing fabulous happens inside of a comfort zone. Repeat that if you have to: *nothing fabulous happens inside of a comfort zone!*

In fact, there is a classic psychological experiment that proves this theory. In 1908, psychologists Robert M. Yerkes and John D. Dodson explained that being in a state of relative comfort creates a steady level of performance. However, to achieve maximum performance (aka become fearless and fabulous), we need to step into a space of relative anxiety, meaning a space where our anxiety is slightly higher than normal and a healthy level of stress has been induced. This space is called "Optimal Anxiety" and it's where we as humans operate at our best.

On the other hand, too much stress causes our performance to suffer, but working just outside of our comfort zone can do wonders for us. It's important to understand the difference and not set unrealistic, wild goals that cause you to freak out and ultimately get nothing done. There is a gentle balance. Get to know what your comfort zone is, and then dance around outside of it for a bit to gauge your stress level. If you feel excited and productive, you're at a good distance from it. If you feel terrified and unproductive, tiptoe back a few steps and try again. Think about a time in your life where doing something a little scary actually energized you. That's what we're striving for here.

FEARLESS & FABULOUS EXERCISE

List the top three most proud moments of your life. Did these moments force you to stretch outside of your comfort zone?

_____

_____

_____

About three years ago, I discovered a blog titled Tales from the Chambre de Bonne. It was an addictive collection of stories from a girl who had a set of balls I could only dream of having. I quickly became hooked on her stories of living in Paris, alone. From her gut-wrenching breakup tales to her hilarious French faux pas, I lived vicariously through Lisa's musings for quite some time before I worked up my own balls to email her. We hit it off and have since become great friends. I asked her to be a part of this book because she inspires me every day with her lust for life and her courageous attitude.

FEARLESS & FABULOUS SUCCESS STORY
"A New Yorker in Paris"
An Essay by Lisa Czarina Michaud
Paris-Based Writer and Blogger at Ellacoquine.com

How powerful is fear to you and would you let it stop you from pursuing ambitions? Would you not launch that dream project out of fear of public failure? Would you not put down those first words out of fear of bad writing? Would you back out of experiencing an exotic destination out of fear of flying? I ask myself these simple questions when inspiration strikes and I see that my fears are trying to talk me out of it.

I have never been one to shy away from a challenge, especially when I was a younger woman. But as I crept towards thirty, the stakes seemed to be higher. It put my last whopper of a dream in question: should I move to Paris by myself?

The idea to move to Paris knocked all of my other experiences out of the ballpark. It wasn't moving to the Pacific Northwest at eighteen-years-old, it certainly was not moving down to Los Angeles to chase down the coveted SAG card, or even working for famous fashion tyrants in Manhattan where I really had something to be scared about every day. This dream involved uprooting my life to a new country, learning a new language, and truly starting afresh, alone.

Along with my own doubts on how I was going to make this happen, friends at the time fed me with an assortment of their fears that they were pawning onto me: "It would be impossible to learn a second language as an adult" or "The unemployment rate is higher in France" or "You'll never get married if you keep moving around" or "Did you know that the euro is stronger than the dollar?" and "The French are rude." Bereft of funds, a job, and proper paperwork were certainly significant factors to consider before making this decision. The other excuses, however, were not. Essentially, these friends were a form of fear, just in cuter outfits.

With two suitcases and a bright outlook, this New Yorker arrived at Charles de Gaulle airport on a sunny morning in September to go see about this dream.

As much as I would like to say that two months later I put all of those naysayers in their place with a settled-in life replete with a dream job, a lively group of friends who helped me learn to sspeak passable French (even if it was with a thick New York accent!) with my polite and loving French man, I can't. It took eight months. And about another eight to completely lose it.

From six thousand miles away, I could feel the silent satisfaction from said "friends" when my Paris life came crashing down on me: the polite and loving French man decided a month after I had given up my apartment to live with him, that he would rather be alone, the lively group of friends disappeared with him, my savings account was thinning out, and I got robbed by someone I knew. Overnight, my French dream had morphed into a total nightmare putting me at yet another crossroads: Do I stay in Paris or go back home?

This is a "Champagne Diet" book, ladies, what do you think I did?

I did end up going back to New York to secure a proper visa that would allow me to work in France. Upon my return, I found a small part-time job, joined a gym, and started a blog to share my stories and experiences with other like-minded women. Because I was placing the focus on helping myself rather than seeking the next rescue, I was unconsciously laying down the foundation of a stronger life in Paris on my own. It's really what I should have done in the first place.

Five years after that fateful first morning at the airport and I'm still in Paris. Can you believe it? I can! I live with my husband (a different guy!) in a quaint apartment near Bastille where I am working on my first novel, work a part-time job, and welcome each day with gratitude. Paris has certainly been more of a struggle than I set out for, but like any true diva, she was worth fighting for.

Lisa knew that pursuing her dream would make her uncomfortable, but she did it anyway. And now she's reaping the benefits (in the form of the most fabulous cheese and wine this world has to offer!) Merci beaucoup for your balls, Lisa. They are an inspiration to all of us.

Laugh at Yourself

I'll never forget the first time I had to speak in public. I was a panelist at a discussion among women entrepreneurs and a room full of at least 100 amazingly talented women surrounded me. Talk about pressure! I was so freaked out about how I looked, what I sounded like, and whether or not I'd make any sense. Before the event, I took deep breaths and tried my hardest to center myself. I went over all the points I wanted to make in my mind, prepared for possible questions that may be asked, and repeated positive affirmations in my head.

When the time came to speak, the moderator started with me, and I completely lost my train of thought. She asked me a question that I did not expect, but rather than get flustered and turn beet red (what the "old me" would have done), I paused, made a joke, and the audience erupted with laughter. Being able to not take myself so seriously broke the ice for all of us, and the vibe of the night immediately shifted from somber and stoic to light-hearted and fun.

You know that quote, "If you embrace your flaws, nobody

39

can use them against you."That has been my guiding star in any would-be embarrassing moment. Owning who you are, flaws and all, is the key to being fearless and fabulous. *Nobody* is perfect. We all forget our lines. We all slip on ice in front of the hot guy. We all spill the entire contents of our purse (including tampons) on the subway. We all have that awkward moment. The trick is embracing it, laughing at yourself, and moving on gracefully.

Baby Steps are Brilliant

No matter what your dream is know that it can absolutely happen if you take baby steps. In fact, baby steps are brilliant. They allow us to gain momentum and the confidence to keep going. Think about dipping your toes into a freezing cold pool. That first dip is super cold, right? But slowly, as you submerge the rest of your foot, the temperature of the water becomes more bearable. Soon enough you are sliding into that pool, barely noticing how chilly it is. It's all about easing in.

Some of the greatest accomplishments start with small steps. Take for example someone who has lost 100 pounds. If they looked at their overall goal in the beginning of their weight loss journey, they probably wouldn't have gotten past day one. But if they look at each day or even each hour as an opportunity to take a step in the right direction, their goal becomes much more manageable. And better yet, we're able to measure success on a smaller scale and celebrate those wins along the way to keep pushing us forward. So break that goal down into baby steps and prove to yourself that you can accomplish whatever you want. Your fear will quickly shrink as you sashay all the way into your dreams.

FEARLESS
&FABULOUS

Nothing fabulous happens inside of a comfort zone.

FIVE

BELIEVE THAT
EVERYTHING IS POSSIBLE

I've always been a dreamer. I spend a lot of time in my own head, fantasizing about the kind of life I want to live. One of my best friends has a running joke with me that I live in a bubble, and she's right, I do! This isn't an insult to me; in fact, I think it's crucial that we all live in a bubble, at least part of the time.

Let me explain.

We live in a world that is tainted with negativity. Just put on the morning news and there's a good chance you'll hear about a murder before you've even had your first sip of coffee. And while you can't tune everything out, you also have to give yourself some healthy space from "reality." And I use the word reality in quotation marks because the reality we've been conditioned to does not have to be the one we live in. Ultimately, we are responsible for designing a world that feels good for us. I'll explain more about that in a minute.

Release the Energy Vampires

Everything around us is energy. From the conversation you have with the clerk at the supermarket, to the music you listen to, to the couple you hear fighting in the apartment above you. We are like a giant sponge, constantly soaking in the energy around us. And if you're not careful, the bad energy can quickly creep in and affect you in a major way.

Do you have someone in your life that just *loves* to burst your bubble? That person who whenever you share your wishes and goals with they come up with a reason why they think it won't work? These people are what I call energy vampires, and they breed fear. They love to discourage dreamers and they love to suck you into their negative worlds. If you're working on becoming a fearless and fabulous woman, you're going to have to seriously limit the time you spend sharing your desires with these types of people. Craft your conversations with them carefully. If they shoot down your dreams, they aren't the right people to share them with.

Your energy vampires love to tell you to "be more realistic." But being "realistic" looks different to everyone. One of the main concepts of the Law of Attraction is that your thoughts become things. You create your reality. So it makes no sense for someone to tell you something can't be done. Sure, maybe it's not realistic in their world, but this is *your* party, sister. You invite who you want and what you want in it.

I once coached a woman (let's call her Marissa) who had the ultimate energy vampire – a negative spouse. Marissa and her husband had been married for thirteen years, and over time he had become more and more toxic. Because he had low self-esteem and was extremely unhappy in his own life, he cut Marissa down at every chance he got. Whenever she would share her success with him, he belittled her and ultimately rattled her confidence and caused her to spiral into a deep depression.

Though it was difficult, Marissa and her husband eventually split up. She decided that she did not deserve to remain in such a negative situation and had to make a very big decision. Was it extremely painful to end her marriage? Absolutely. Did she doubt her decision a thousand times? She sure did. But the pain of living with someone who not only drained her energy, but emotionally abused her was so much worse. Marissa took control of her life (by believing in and using the strategies in this book!) and eventually built back up her self-esteem. She is now happier, more successful and more confident than ever.

Right now, commit to releasing all energy vampires from your life. Commit to letting go of anyone that does not fully support you and help lift you higher. Do not let anyone who drains you or muddies up your spirit take up room in your precious mind or your physical space. You have one life to live, and you deserve nothing but the best people in it.

Create Your Own Reality

When I first read *The Secret*, I felt as if I had already been living this way for years. The Law of Attraction had been my guide for most of my life and I didn't even know it. For the most part, I have always felt that anything was possible as long as I could envision it, work hard, and believe that it could happen. This type of thinking has allowed me to accomplish many of my dreams, and has given me the courage to keep plugging away at the things I know will happen in time.

My friends always tell me, "Cara, you always make things happen. If you say you're going to accomplish something, I never doubt you'll do it." And one of the main reasons I am able to do that is because I can truly visualize my desires coming true. I focus all of my energy on what I want and I don't spend any precious time wondering what will happen if it doesn't work out. Does everything I want always happen exactly as I envision it?

Of course not! But I don't view anything as a failure. I just view it as a sign that I need to tweak a few things and try a new way. And you can do the exact same thing.

As you read this book, I want you to believe that you are the ultimate designer of your future. Much like the Law of Attraction says, your thoughts create your reality. So know that your mind is powerful beyond measure. When you subscribe to this way of thinking, fear disappears. It's impossible to be afraid when you have an unwavering faith that everything will work out exactly as it should.

This mindset takes practice, but it's entirely possible to train yourself to operate on a fearless and fabulous frequency at all times.

FEARLESS & FABULOUS EXERCISE

Answer these questions in your journal or below.

In my fearless & fabulous reality, I am capable of:

I will not let the following things distract me from living my best life:

Have Faith in the Universe

No matter what your religion is, I bet you probably have some sort of faith in something. Whether it's God, or The Universe, it's hard to deny that there is a divine force working around us at all times. The sooner you can believe that, the sooner you will become fearless. Why? Because that divine force is working in your favor. The Universe embraces fearless and fabulous women because they are the ones living their truth!

One of the biggest reasons we are fearful is because we assume we're not going to get what we want. But guess what? There is so much sparkly, fabulous goodness in this world that it's *impossible* for you not to get your share of it. In fact, you can have as much of it as you want because there is an endless supply. The Universe is abundant. There is more than enough for everyone. So that crap you're afraid of? Get over it! Amazing things are waiting for you. You just have to build up the courage to go grab them.

The trick is to cultivate a sense of faith so strong that nothing breaks it. If you truly believe with every fiber of your being that everything you want will come to you, you will be unstoppable. We get caught up in fear when we begin to overanalyze and overthink things. So give up those behaviors that do not serve you and believe that your life will be nothing short of amazing.

FEARLESS & FABULOUS SUCCESS STORY
An Essay by Kelly Barkhurst
Party Planner Extraordinaire at Ohkellys.com

My all time favorite quote is this: "We do not remember days, we remember moments." - Cesare Paves.

Every single one of us has moments that are vivid in our memories ... our lives are made up of them, each one piling on top of the others. Some are made up of pure joy and happiness and some are tragic and full of deep sorrow. Happy or heart wrenching, they have the power to define our days and we remember them with great clarity.

My most defining moment in life was on November 5, 1978 when both my mother and father were killed in a plane accident. I was eleven years old. This is by far the most heartbreaking event of my life and in many ways defines me and who I am today. It is a rare day that I don't think about my parents and miss them terribly, but I am not a victim of this accident. In the midst of my sadness, I choose to be thankful for the short time I had with them and realize that every moment is precious and fleeting. It is up to us to appreciate and celebrate the life we have rather than fear it and also celebrate the people who are a part of it when we have them, because "this too shall pass". My parents' death taught me this.

My second favorite quote is: "The things you are passionate about are not random, they are your calling."

More than anything else, I love to create events, plan parties, and bake fabulous cakes and desserts. This runs deep in me and I cannot even tell you how ridiculously excited I get about helping you plan a party. However, I have always just thought that this passion was a hobby and it wasn't until recently I realized it's the gift I have been given and that I should cultivate it and share it with others. We are all given special gifts and talents and I believe with all my heart that it's our job to share them. This doesn't mean we're not afraid.

After a lot of thinking and planning, I launched my company Oh Kelly's this year, because I finally realized that I wanted to spend my life helping people create their own special moments. I am passionate about creating moments for people that they will remember, helping them mark a moment with something special and helping them celebrate a loved one. Life is what we make of it and I want to spread as much joy as possible.

FEARLESS
& FABULOUS

It's impossible to be afraid when you have an unwavering faith
that everything will work out exactly as it should.
Cultivate this faith every single day.

SIX
LET GO OF THE PAST

*"We can't become what we need to be
by remaining what we are."*
— Oprah Winfrey

Have you ever tried something and failed? Of course you have! That's why you're fearful in the first place. When things don't go the way we expect them to, it's easy to throw in the towel and never take a chance again. Our pasts can either define us or develop us. If our pasts define us, that means a determination has been made and there's no chance for growth. But if we allow our pasts to develop us, we are able to learn from our experiences and gain invaluable wisdom and perspective.

One of the main causes of fear is a lack of past success. Think about it: if you've racked up an impressive portfolio of "wins" then most likely you're confident enough to pursue your dreams fearlessly because you have proof that you can accomplish them. But that isn't the case for most people. We all make mistakes and experience perceived "failures"; that's part of life. Unfortunately, we can't rewrite history, but we can begin taking small steps that will ultimately lead us to success. Every move in the right direction can be celebrated as an accomplishment.

Let's imagine you want to write a book. Maybe up until this point, you've been unsuccessful in completing it. Right now, I want you to focus on the tiny steps that will ultimately add up to a finished manuscript. Let's say you've researched similar books in your genre, written down a few rough ideas, and came up with a title. You may not realize it, but those actions are moving you toward your ultimate goal. The more we view those steps as successes, the more confidence we gain. And confidence builds momentum.

FEARLESS & FABULOUS EXERCISE

Think about some goals you've been working on. Write down every small success you've achieved up to this point.

_____

_____

_____

_____

_____

_____

_____

Focus on What You Want Now

In case you haven't noticed, I make a lot of references to *The Secret* and The Law of Attraction in this book. One of the major concepts taught in The Law of Attraction is that when you focus on what you want, you get more of it, and what you don't want falls away. Of course, as the Law goes, the opposite is true as well. If you focus on what you don't want, you get more of that.

So let's take for example a past failure. Let's say your last relationship fell apart. If you spend all of your time focusing on what went wrong, how you and your former partner behaved in that relationship, and how you don't want a repeat of that relationship, chances are that's exactly what you'll get. You will be so obsessed with looking at the past that you'll project it onto the future. Come on, we've all done it! You blame the potential new guy for everything the past guy did. You assume that all guys are jerks because the last one cheated, or you assume that you'll never meet a man who puts your needs first because none of the past ones have. But if you wipe the slate clean in your mind and live life with fresh eyes and an open heart, focusing on everything you do want in a new relationship, you will get exactly that. So spend your time thinking about what you want now, and forget the rest.

Remember, you are the "haute couture" designer of your life. It's on you to make it as fabulous and extraordinary as you want it to be. You can choose to keep reliving past failures, or decide to keep going and create something amazing. Eventually, you will succeed as long as you follow these powerful strategies to get you there. Fearless and fabulous women do not live in the past; they spend their energy creating the future. As Lisa Nichols from *The Secret* says, "You are the designer of your destiny. You are the author. You write the story. The pen is in your hand, and the outcome is whatever you choose." Choose wisely.

Schedule Your Pity Party

Now, don't get me wrong, we aren't fembots. It's completely natural to feel bad over a past failure. We are sensitive, emotional creatures. That's part of what makes us so beautiful. But it's not natural to obsess over that failure. The longer we focus on what went wrong and how badly we feel that we didn't accomplish something, the longer we stay stuck. And in case you haven't noticed, being fearless and fabulous is all about moving forward and taking action. Whenever I work with clients who are trying to move past disappointment, I recommend they give themselves a "mourning period." Whether it is a few hours, or a full day, I encourage them to utilize that time to feel badly and have their pity party, but when the time is up they must move on. By assigning a mourning period, we get it out of our system and then emerge with a recharged outlook.

A few years ago, I started making collages using mixed media. I used beautiful paper, selected a quote, and then designed each collage, which I then framed. I made a few for myself, and then friends started asking for them. Since they were becoming popular, I thought it might be a good idea to sell these framed collages, so I created an Etsy shop. When they started selling out, I went a step further and approached a few boutiques, which also took them to sell. In two month's time, I had signed up for a huge local fair and sold my creations at my own booth. I absolutely loved designing these collages. It was my therapy and a brand new creative outlet that I truly enjoyed. But even though they were selling like hot cakes, I wasn't making any money on them. In fact, I was losing money. The frames were expensive as was the shipping, and ultimately it was not proving to be the profitable business I had hoped it would be. It was hard to make the decision to put my efforts elsewhere, especially since I designed a website, logo, and business cards, but I ultimately decided to close down the business.

I remember taking that weekend to grieve. I was sad because I had found so much joy in creating art that people loved, but ultimately I made peace with the fact that it was not sustainable. I closed down my Etsy shop, packed away the remainder of my stock, and moved on. Could I have let this "failure" prevent me from ever starting another business? Absolutely. But instead I let it go and moved onto something else that inspired me.

FEARLESS & FABULOUS SUCCESS STORY
An Essay by Keryl Pesce
Author, *Happy Bitch* at Happy-bitch.com

"I don't care. I love you. I love you, baby, and I'm going to be with you."

Hearing my husband say these words was a powerful turning point in my life – a moment when I was being truly blessed and given a gift that would forever change the course of my life. The gratitude I feel for these words today is immense and something I reflect on often.

What's the big deal? Why are they so powerful and meaningful? Allow me to put this in perspective for you.

I grew up, as most girls do, with the goal of marrying the man of my dreams, of being married once, being a devoted wife and living happily ever after. So after six years into the relationship and finally deciding to get married, my dream came true. Five years later, it came to a crashing end as I walked up behind my husband to hear him say the above to someone else.

I can unequivocally tell you that the moment I heard those words brought forth an absolute low point in my life filled with such immense fear and pain, so deep in my heart, I was certain a piece of it, if not most of it, had died. The fact is, hearts do die - in pieces and sometimes as a whole emotionally as heartbreak and physically as a heart attack. . And when this happens, while it doesn't always claim a life completely, there is some irreparable damage. It simply can't be undone.

55

So how lucky are we, really, when the pain of a perceived failure, whether it be a job, business venture, or relationship, doesn't permanently damage our hearts? Not only are our hearts not damaged, they grow stronger. Show me a strong, vibrant, caring woman and I promise she has a story to share that at one time, wasn't so pretty. She is the powerhouse she is because of the strength she gained from her past.

As low as that point was in my life, I can equally be strong in my statement that I am now the happiest I've ever been, married to an amazing man who's every thought, decision and move are with my happiness in mind. And vice versa.

No one can tell you or anyone else how long it will take to get over a perceived negative event, but anyone who has triumphed over one or two or a hundred will tell you the key to getting there faster lies in changing the questions you ask. The sooner you go from "Why me?" to "What's next? What do I now want? What good can come from this?" the sooner you'll thrive.

None of us need wish our pasts were different. It's impossible to change. But every single one of us can choose to change how we see it and not only diminish its negative power over us, but leverage it to create something more beautiful and fabulous that would never have been an available option, had we not gone through it.

The only power the past has over you is the power you choose to give it. Letting go of regret, forgiving yourself, other people and circumstances not only releases you from its grips, it fills you with a newfound power. One you own, always. It's simply up to you to see it, grab onto it and share it with the world.

Much love and happiness to you always.
Keryl Pesce

FEARLESS & FABULOUS

The past does not define me. Every day is a fresh start to be the "haute couture" designer of my new and fabulous reality.

SEVEN
EMBRACE FEAR

"We gain strength, and courage, and confidence by each experience in which we really stop to look fear in the face ... we must do that which we think we cannot."
— *Eleanor Roosevelt*

Let's be honest. Fear is scary. The unknown is exactly that: unknown. And that can be a terrifying thought. It's totally natural to feel fearful. In fact, it's important. Fear lets us know something is at risk. Whether it's the fear we feel as a child before touching a hot pan that our mother warned would burn us, or the fear we feel before giving our two week's notice at our job in order to change our career path, fear is a real feeling that should be respected and embraced. The sooner we meet our fears with open arms and embrace them lovingly, the sooner we will be able to watch them disappear.

The first step in embracing fear is acknowledging it. Think of the areas in your life where you fear fearful. You're probably so used to tucking your fear away and trying to ignore it that you may not even realize where it exists (I used to be a pro at ignoring fear; it's totally common). But really dig deep and examine where fear crops up for you. Once you've done this, get comfortable with becoming present to it. You may even want to say out loud, "I'm afraid of X" or write it down in your journal.

After you've acknowledged your fear, start to gently embrace it. You can even express gratitude for it. Like I said above, our fears are not a *bad* thing. Fear is like a big, flashing, neon pink sign that says: "Hey you! Something big is going on here! Check it out!" So be grateful for your fears, and greet them with kindness. The quicker we embrace our fears, the quicker we can disarm them and take away their hold on us. When you stop fighting something, you immediately take away its power.

FEARLESS & FABULOUS EXERCISE

In what area of your life can you embrace fear?

_____

_____

_____

Reap the Rewards

Last year, I planned a solo trip to London and Paris. A caveat to this story is that I used to be terrified of flying. I'm talking grip-your-seat, ask –the-flight-attendants-if-they-smell-smoke, heart-palpitations scared. Whenever I traveled somewhere, I spent the weeks leading up to that trip paralyzed with anxiety and fear over the upcoming flight. In fact, it ruined most vacations for me because even though I made it to my destination, I obsessed over the flight home so I rarely enjoyed the time I was away.

But last year, something changed for me. My desire to travel to London and Paris suddenly greatly outweighed my fear of flying – and flying alone. You know those moments in life where you suddenly feel this superwoman-like strength and decide to create a situation for yourself to thrive in? It's almost like I set this trip up to prove to myself that I could do it. It was a learning experience, business trip, and vacation all wrapped into one.

If you know me, then you know that my business is my baby. I created *The Champagne Diet®* six years ago, and in that time what started as a little unknown blog has grown into a full-blown brand and business filled with amazing clients, books, workshops, and more. And it just so happens because of the magic of the Internet, many of my clients, readers, and friends are based outside of the US. So when a few of my UK clients and readers began asking when I'd be on their side of the pond, I knew I wanted to make a trip of it. London is my absolute favorite city in the world, and I hop on any chance to travel there. And what's London without Paris? I mean come on, a two-hour train ride to the Eiffel tower? How can a gal say no?

As my trip began to take shape, I chatted with Paris-based writer Lisa Czarina (whose story you read earlier), and we decided to throw a soiree to mark my first trip to the City of Light. We worked with a local luxury vacation rental company, secured a fabulous apartment in the heart of Paris to throw our party in, and began planning (we're Italian girls; any excuse to eat and drink, right?) With a guest list overflowing with Paris' most fabulous bloggers and entrepreneurs, my plane and train tickets booked, and hotel secured, this trip was *on*.

The weeks leading up to my trip were filled with a mix of anxiety and excitement. I watched fear of flying videos on YouTube, tracked countless Virgin Atlantic flights to prove to myself they actually take off and land safely every day (what a concept, right?) and practiced deep breathing techniques. I relentlessly tried to brainwash myself into not being afraid to fly halfway across the world by myself. Although some of those tactics worked to calm me down temporarily, the truth was, in the back of my mind, I was still scared. Even though the fear was real, every time I felt it, I shifted my focus to the excitement of my trip. I looked photos of Paris online, planned my outfits, and thought about all the amazing people I was about to meet.

The morning of my flight I was so entrenched in nervousness that I didn't even drink coffee because I was worried it would make me too jittery (and me skipping coffee is like the Earth not rotating. It just does *not* happen). I remember getting to the airport and having a glass of champagne. And then having another glass. And then having another. As we boarded the plane, I could feel my heart race. Even a couple of glasses of bubbly couldn't calm me down. Still, I embraced the fear I felt and got on the plane. And you know what? I was fine. Was I uncomfortable? Absolutely. I mean, who can be totally at-ease while hovering 30,000 feet above the Earth!? But little by little, I felt better and before I knew it, I had landed in London. And I felt like a million bucks.

By embracing my fear of flying and doing it anyway, I was able to conquer it. The fear wasn't gone; I simply refused to let it control me. Suddenly, my fear no longer had power. I wasn't paralyzed; I was liberated. It's all about pushing ourselves past that point of discomfort. If you can accomplish that, the reward will be greater than you can imagine.

FEARLESS & FABULOUS SUCCESS STORY
An Essay by Victoria James
Thestylejournal.co.uk

I don't remember traveling to the airport that day ... for me, flying was just a means to an end, like getting in the car, or catching a train. I loved the anticipation of discovering a new corner of the world ... but I never remembered any of the journey. There was nothing to take any notice of, an insignificant part of a day. Just like I don't remember brushing my teeth, or my first cup of tea in the morning.

I had always had a sense of excitement for any trip whether with family, friends or on my own and had a very deep-rooted wanderlust which was never far from my mind, but the actual flying part never registered as anything other than a way to get somewhere else.

That day however, I do remember stepping into the tunnel leading to the plane, walking hand-in-hand with the man I had fallen crazy-in-love with towards the means that would take us to our first romantic holiday together ... and I was suddenly petrified. A wave of unexplainable, crippling fear washed over me. I had never experienced anything like it in my life.

I was always such a free-spirited person. No cares or worries, always looking forward to the next amazing thing that I knew was right around every corner so I had no way to explain these feelings to this guy smiling at me like he knew this was to be the first of many fabulous holidays together. So I kept my mouth shut, panicked like crazy inside myself and felt like the whole world was inexplicably caving in around me.

Being rather blasé about things I buried it. Didn't think about any of my feelings and just thought that by the time our next holiday came around I'd be over it.

In the mean time, we saved up and bought a house together, planned the most amazing wedding, partied until the sun came up and knew our honeymoon would be just what we needed after eighteen months of wedding planning and career changes.

We collected our luggage, arrived at the airport, went to board and there it was again. Like a huge slap in my just-married glowing face.

FEAR.

I couldn't believe it. I was freaking out inside again. The only thing keeping me going was the thought of hot sun and two weeks of just us.

We had a beautiful time, but the thought of flying home again was never far from my mind and I was a nervous mess.

After our honeymoon came Paris, then Amsterdam and the fear got worse every time so I resigned myself to the fact holidays just weren't for me and locked the feelings away. I couldn't stand the embarrassment of talking about it, never mind how I cringe at the memory of asking the poor cabin crew member on the Amsterdam flight if I was going to die that day. Awful – just awful.

That was nearly ten years ago. In this time, my husband's career has seen him spend a lot of time all over Europe, Japan, Brazil, India and Thailand. Every time he went away I would be beside myself with a mix of anxiety for his flight and envy that he was able to see these amazing places and I felt I couldn't go, which then made me furious with myself. My wanderlust has never gone – I just locked it away.

So this new year, aware that I was about to turn 35, I decided enough was enough. Surely by 35 a girl is supposed to have her shit together?

I have a gorgeous life and genuinely feel blessed every day. I have my own businesses which I love and feel fulfilled in most areas ... but I haven't stepped foot out the UK in nearly ten years.

In this time, I've avoided facing up to my fear. Using reasons like, "Oh, we're moving house, we can't holiday this year" or "No, I just started a business so I can't take time away from that" and my best/most ridiculous yet ...

"I just had to have the limited edition Gucci bag so a holiday is definitely off the cards."

Yes, I actually said those words out loud. (I do love that bag though – it just gets better with age).

Anyway ...

Time for change, so I decided to get to know myself and think about who I am so I can build myself into the person I envisaged I would he at 35

We're also coming up to our 10th wedding anniversary this year and I cannot face the thought of not celebrating it in style. We both deserve a magnificent holiday to relax and unwind so I had to get over myself and face up to my fear ...

There's a guy I know of who practices hypnotherapy, and having decided I wanted to get to the root of my problem rather than cover it with pills, I decided to get in touch. I see him in passing every month or so as his wife has a salon just near my boutique. The next time I saw him, I decided to go from a friendly smile to a verbal interaction. I could do this. So, putting the law of attraction to play, I visualized bumping into him and asking for his help. I literally couldn't believe it when parking my car up the very next day, he came walking by. It was meant to be. So I spoke to him and honestly, it was the best thing I've done.

A couple of weeks later I found myself sat in his office talking through my fear of flying, while he asked about other general areas of my lifestyle, career and down-time.

Turns out, I had allowed this fear to limit myself so much so that when I looked back at opportunities I had let pass me by, I just knew I had to take control of this and if hypnotherapy was a solution, then I was willing to give it a try.

I just needed the desire to address it and he would be able to give me the tools required to solve the problem. Christian's mantra is "What the mind believes, you will achieve."

He explained that the process we were about to go through was not an over-ride of my own feelings – he wouldn't be telling me "You're not afraid of flying anymore." It has to come from within yourself, so during the hypnosis you do a lot of visualisation and this process begins to realign your thinking and feelings towards the issue.

We were going to turn my 'Fear of Flying' dial down from maximum to an acceptable, reasonable level, and turn up my 'Confidence to Fly' dial from minimum to as high as I wanted it to go. It's about making the two parts of your brain work together in the right way again. The part of your brain that tells you you're afraid is the same part of the brain that remembers automatic function such as how to walk, how to drive, how to use a knife and fork. You don't re-learn these things every day, they are remembered.

This part of my brain was remembering and reminding me that I was afraid of flying – something that I just needed to process through and remember isn't actually a threat. It was a learned reaction which could have started from something totally unrelated, like a stressful situation coupled with a plane journey which means your brain could then associate flying with feeling stressed.

Looking back, that first time I felt frightened was at a very stressful time in my life. I just thought I was okay because I was about to go on holiday. It would make sense for this to have been my trigger.

Being hypnotized is like a relaxing, blissed-out super-charged sleep – but I was conscious, my mind full of vibrant, moving images right there in front of me while all the time feeling cocooned in the marshmallow comfort of his reclining chair. Cosy, safe, happy and I was left feeling refreshed, super-smiley and knowing I was able to achieve anything.

So after a couple of sessions, I did it. My 35th birthday came around, along with my goal of getting back to Paris. This was it.

Due to my husband's frequent flying we were able to use the BA lounge at Heathrow, so at 5am that Saturday morning we were sat with a glass of gin, eating a delicious breakfast, waiting to board our flight with my renewed confidence in flying and it felt fabulous! Don't get me wrong, I was nervous, but at the same time empowered that I was taking control of a fear that has held me back for years equipped with the tools I had learned to control my thoughts.

Getting off the plane at the other end was not the high I imagined it to be. I was very calm, no emotional spike. Just like I was undoing my seatbelt in the car ready to get on with my day. This left me feeling confused ...

Paris was amazing. We packed in every minute of our time there and I loved it but the flat feeling remained – I wanted a high but it was no where to be found!

    I realised, this is exactly how I was supposed to feel. There was no elation, because why would there be? I flew. I was on holiday. That was it. Bit of an anti-climax really after all that fuss for the last 10 years. I can admit to feeling a little disappointed, but happy that I had done it.

    Then it came to flying home, Sunday evening, back in the airport lounge and I was feeling terrified. What was this all about?! I could not believe this was happening. I didn't even get excited about the free champagne in the lounge so I knew something was amiss. I LOVE champagne and I take any excuse to break a bottle open!

    Boarding our flight was very difficult for me, however the cabin crew were amazing, they took the time to talk to me, inviting me to speak to the pilots before take off and all of a sudden I felt totally calm again. Like someone had waved a wand and magically swiped the fear away. The wave of fear that came all those years ago withdrew and I felt like a weight had been lifted off my body. My chest and shoulders relaxed, my hands stopped feeling hot and I was smiling ear to ear.

    I took my seat, remembered my tools and I can say with absolute certainty, I LOVED every second of that flight. Take off was exhilarating and I even spent time looking out the window enjoying the view.

    It was everything I had hoped I would feel and more! This was the high I had been missing on the way over. The excitable traveller my husband had never seen before was back and I WAS LOVING IT!

    The captain invited me to talk to him and the co-pilot again after we landed so I could ask questions and he could speak to me about our journey and I cannot tell you how happy I was. I felt like an excitable child giving hugs and kisses to the crew and the pilots. I had done it! My fear is GONE! I LOVE flying again and I cannot wait to get booked onto my next flight so I can get this free spirit back out that has been away for so long.

    My third session with Christian was booked five days after we returned, like a de-brief session and it turns out the flat feelings encountered on the way out were to be entirely expected. This trip has been ten years in the making, all that anticipation, time and anxiety needed to be processed with my newly learned thought processes and realigned back to where they should be. The feeling of a low before boarding was my brain re-assessing what my feelings were and processing them to feel real and accurate again with the help of reason and positive experience, then the high upon landing back in the UK was the proof that I'm over it – I can do it.

There is no need to feel afraid. This is perfectly safe and a completely normal thing to do and with that, the thought processing was complete.

That was the high. The knowing it was right, and I am capable of turning my fears around using the tools I am equipped with to face a fearful situation and do it anyway.

I feel fantastic every day and can apply the skills learned to any situation which feels uncomfortable or unnerving. My life has been changed and I could not be happier – the high stays with me.

I learned from this, just because you are frightened doesn't mean anything bad is going to happen. It's a simple choice whether you enjoy what you are about to do or let yourself be afraid.

Perhaps it is our feelings towards flying and passion for bubbly that makes Victoria and I such kindred spirits. Whatever it is, I can honestly tell you that she is one fabulous woman (with a great fashion sense, to boot!) Her story should inspire you to never give up tackling those fears – and help you realize that doing so is not always a quick fix. Victoria continued to challenge her fear even when it seemed to keep cropping up. She is about to celebrate her tenth wedding anniversary in Greece and I could not be happier for her. I'll be waving at you from the ground, Victoria, champagne in hand!

FEARLESS
&FABULOUS

By embracing fear, I take away its power over me.

EIGHT
REDEFINE FAILURE

"Success is most often achieved by those
who don't know that failure is inevitable."
— *Coco Chanel*

I'm going to let you in on one of the biggest secrets of fearless and fabulous women: we don't believe in failure. Think about it — fear would not exist if failure didn't. We're scared to take chances because we don't want to fail. But what if you redefined your definition of failure? To me, failure is just a sign that I need to redirect my energy. Something didn't work out one way, so I need to try a new way. This is how I've eliminated fear from my life. And it's made everything feel possible.

Our society has done a great job at making us feel shameful about failure. We live in a highly competitive world where it's all about winning. We are taught that we are incapable and worthless if we do not succeed at something. That attitude does nothing for us but keep us face-down and make us even more fearful.

But what if you viewed your perceived failures as powerful learning experiences? When you fail, you simply eliminate one way of doing something, which leads you closer to success. You're just figuring out ways that don't work for you. The trick is to keep it moving so you can discover the way that does work. Thomas Edison said it best when asked about his initial failures before finally inventing the light bulb. He simply replied: "I have not failed. I've just found 10,000 ways that won't work."

A few months ago, I partnered with a spa to roll out a five-week long group-coaching workshop. The spa directors were so excited to feature this workshop since it would be the biggest one they'd ever had. We planned every detail for weeks leading up to the event. We promoted on social media, I personally invited friends and clients, I dropped off flyers all over the neighborhood, and we even planned a major kick-off event. And guess what? Not one person signed up. Could I have viewed this as a massive failure? Could I have been completely embarrassed that my idea did not pan out? Of course! I was disappointed, but I was not discouraged. I quickly put my thinking tiara on and came up with an even more fabulous series of workshops that would require less of a commitment from clients. I refused to give up; instead, I devised a new and improved way to offer my services to the spa. And this time around, I had even more ideas than the first time. I viewed a would-be "failure" as an opportunity to innovate and improve.

Rather than looking at a failure as a negative experience, look for the lesson. How can that experience empower you? What can you take away from it to make you a better, stronger, and more prepared person the next time around?

FEARLESS & FABULOUS EXERCISE

Think about one of your past "failures" and look for the opportunity in it. How did you grow from the experience?

_____

_____

_____

Famous Failures

Did you know that some of the most successful people failed
first? Oprah Winfrey was told she wasn't "made for TV" when
she first started her career. She got her first television gig at
Baltimore's WJZ-TV as an on-air anchor, and less than eight
months into the job she was pulled from that position and given
lower-level responsibilities. Beethoven's music teacher once told
him he was a hopeless composer. Walt Disney was fired from a
newspaper after being told he lacked good ideas. John Grisham's
first novel was rejected by sixteen agents and twelve publishing
houses (I feel ya, John!). The first time Jerry Seinfeld ever took
the stage to do stand-up comedy, he was booed off because he
panicked and froze. Stephen King's first book, Carrie, was rejected thirty times, causing him to scrap the manuscript. His
wife fished it out of the trash and it went on to become one of
his many best-selling books. The one common denominator of
all these so-called "failures?" They never gave up.

Don't Be Afraid to Look Silly

For some reason, most of us women are serious perfection-
ists. We are so damn afraid to look silly that we hold ourselves

back from so much. Here's a little secret: *nobody* is perfect! Some of the most fabulous women that I admire have made mistakes – some that I've witnessed, some that they've told me about. Do I think any less of them? Of course not! If there is one glaring quality that all fearless and fabulous women possess it is that they are not afraid to look silly. I truly can't stress that enough.

Having the guts to make mistakes and "fail" is part of the process in gaining confidence. The more you let go, the less embarrassed you feel if something doesn't go as planned. So what if you totally screw something up? Own it. Your confidence will inspire someone else to take a chance. It's like a domino effect of empowerment.

&FEARLESS &FABULOUS

Fear would not exist if failure didn't.
Redefine your definition of failure and look for
opportunities to stretch and grow.

NINE
DETACH FROM THE OUTCOME

Wouldn't life be grand if we knew that every chance we took would give us the results we wanted? I don't know about you, but I would have taken every leap possible without a single doubt. But how boring would that be? When things don't go the way we plan, it's a chance to learn. There is always a lesson planted deep within every experience, even if it takes a while to uncover it.

Detaching from the outcome is only possible if you have faith in the Universe, as I outlined in the previous chapters. When we wholeheartedly believe that everything is working in our favor, we can let go of the details of exactly *how* something should turn out for us. Think of a time in your life where you really, really wanted something. Maybe you took an exam and you were anxiously awaiting the results to see if you passed. Your energy was filled with fear and doubt because you were worried there was a chance you may have failed. By projecting that energy onto the outcome, you filled yourself with negative emotion. And fearless and fabulous women do not operate on that frequency!

As I mentioned earlier, one of my biggest life lessons came when I decided to self-publish my first book, *Sparkle*. I spent years attached to an outcome. I wanted so badly to be traditionally published that I saw no other way of my dream become a reality. I was so rigid in my thinking that it catapulted me into a constant state of fear and anxiety. Whenever an email came in from my literary agent, I felt a tightening in my chest. I was terrified of bad news. I put all the power in the hands of editors and allowed these people to control my fate (or so I thought). You can imagine the negative energy that consumed me on a daily basis.

It wasn't until I detached from the outcome that I began to see clearly and free myself from those chains that had bound me for so long. Once I decided to let go of my original plan, a new plan surfaced almost immediately. I saw opportunity in the unexpected and took the power back. I detached from the outcome I expected and wound up with one that surpassed my every hope and desire.

FEARLESS & FABULOUS EXERCISE

Write down an outcome you need to detach from.

_____

_____

_____

Detachment Brings Power

The more attached you are to an outcome, the less power you have. The thought that a circumstance or a thing can bring you happiness sets you up for a position of powerlessness. Let's use dating as an example. We've all been there: we're waiting for our phone to buzz and for that text message to appear from the guy we've become just *mildly* obsessed with. He's perfect in our eyes, and a simple "Hello" from him can turn our whole day around. In that moment, we are attached to an outcome. We're putting so much weight on whether or not we receive that text that we're allowing it to control our mood and ultimately our life. The moment you detach from the outcome, you take back the power. You're able to find happiness regardless of whether or not Mr. Hottie contacts you. Your detachment from his actions brings you freedom and control.

Let's dial back to Chapter Three for a moment. Remember, fearless and fabulous women exude confidence. And confidence just does not work when we have a strong attachment to outcome. If we're depending on something else to make us feel good, we're anxious and insecure because if we don't get it, we know we will feel bad. So the quicker you detach from outcome, the quicker you will build up your confidence. See how these strategies all work together?

Embrace the Unexpected

Living fearlessly means you'll need to get comfortable with the unexpected. The more you take chances, the more you make yourself vulnerable to new and interesting outcomes. Notice I used the word "interesting"? Like I mentioned earlier, how boring would life be if always knew what was going to happen? Learn to start viewing your life as an adventure. Each twist and turn is an opportunity to learn something new about yourself and evolve as a person.

Fearless and fabulous women are flexible. They go with the flow and think on their beautifully pedicured toes. Just because they have mastered the art of going after what they want, doesn't mean they always get the results they hoped for. Life is filled with uncertainty, and the sooner you can practice adapting to that uncertainty, the sooner you will grow. You will become more creative and seek out new opportunities in those moments. That's the beauty of detaching: there's always something new to learn when the Universe hands you something you didn't anticipate.

FEARLESS & FABULOUS TESTIMONIAL
By Rachelle Walker

When I started my business, Mérenity Wellness Studio, I knew it wasn't going to be easy. There is no shortage of statistics on how many start-ups fail, yet for some reason in the beginning I was able to just forge full-steam ahead without much regard for how hard it was actually going to be. I knew I had a "to-do" list miles long but I began each morning with that first wave of "entrepreneurial bliss" knowing that if I tackled one item at a time there was no way I wouldn't be successful!

Then about six months in things began to change. Everything became more real – I was looking at signing a long-term lease for over $100K a year, I would have to hire a complete staff to make the studio a reality and, as always, there was no guarantee I would be able to attract my customers away from their current studios. Would I be able to find reliable staff? Could I hire instructors in the specific disciplines I needed? Was I too young to be trying to take on so much and would no one take me seriously?

On paper I come across as an "ideal" candidate to start a business: both my parents have started successful companies and I grew up with their examples, sometimes working in their businesses. I myself have an MBA and worked for a successful start-up company for almost three years before trying my hand at doing it myself. But there was one thing that no amount of education or experience could help me with – I am your stereotypical Type-A personality control freak. I prefer to sit back, gather information and make a conscious, knowledgeable decision no matter how big or how small. But let me tell you rule #1 I've learned in business – this is not always an option, in fact it rarely is. You have to be comfortable moving forward with maybe only 80% (if you're lucky) of the information.

Being able to detach and step back from my business has been a rollercoaster for me over the past year. In the beginning I was riding high and knew that no matter what happened it would be ok – that I could handle it – and if it didn't work out, so what? I could always start over, it wasn't going to define who I was and if it were meant to be it would be. I loved compiling my business plan, all the research, analysis, development of marketing and financials was something that I could put my hands on and physically control. After years of being in school this was something I absolutely knew how to do – research and evaluate – so while I was in my comfort zone I was able to feel in control. Looking back I believe this is what gave me that original boost of confidence at the start.

Then came the hard part, signing my name on the dotted line of some of these more difficult choices. This is where I could start feeling a loss of control over my surroundings and the outcomes. It was the low point of my ride. We ran into problems with the lease negotiations so they were put on hold, my marketing was taking longer than expected and I wasn't happy that I still had no logo, business cards or website to show anyone my company was real. I didn't realize it at first, but all these smaller issues were starting to add up and weigh heavily on me. I started to freak out and felt that my coveted "timeline for success" was falling apart. All the downtime left me with nothing else to do but agonize over all the possible outcomes and I felt the business was consuming me. The doors weren't even open yet and I was already unable to mentally step back from it. Something had to change. I did not want to be one of those owners that did nothing else but eat, sleep and breathe their businesses and not exists outsides of its success or failure.

It has taken a conscious effort on my part to climb back up that long rollercoaster lift and get back to the top of the hill. First off, I had to acknowledge and accept that the need to be in control is just part of who I am. I've created different outlets for myself, outside of the business, that allows me to remember that regardless of the outcome I am still my own person. Some of what has worked for me was to start a blog to track not only my business process but other interest like cooking, yoga and my upcoming wedding. I've picked up a meditation practice that I use when things start to feel out of control and I feel a complete meltdown is on its way. And I try to do something new everyday (or at least each week) that makes me uncomfortable or provides a challenge as a simple reminder that I don't have to be perfect, I don't have to have all the answers right now and that it will be okay, no matter what.

&FEARLESS
FABULOUS

I view my life as an adventure. The more I detach from the outcome of things, the more power I take back.

TEN
CHANNEL YOUR INNER MUSE

So let's recap what I've covered so far. Up to this point, I've taught you nine powerful strategies to help you overcome your fears: you've learned to decide what you want, own your desires, get confident, get uncomfortable, believe that everything is possible, let go of the past, embrace fear, redefine failure, and detach from the outcome. And now I'm going to let you in on the #1 secret to being a fearless and fabulous woman: channeling your inner muse. What's an inner muse, you may be wondering? It's that woman deep inside of you who gives you all of your creativity, drive, and passion. It's that woman who is so sure of who she is and what she wants, that nothing can get in her way. It's the woman who is pure in her intentions with herself and others. It's the woman who is capable of anything. It's the woman who trusts the Universe completely, and operates on a frequency of positivity at all times. It's your core essence, your truest being. It is your inspiration. *It is your muse.*

Your inner muse is not a wild, erratic mess. She is not nervous, or fearful. Although she is powerful and determined, she is not overworked to the point of exhaustion. She's not filled with stress and anxiety. Instead, she effortlessly glides toward her destiny with confidence, grace and ease. She handles challenges with poise and never gets caught up in her own mind when things don't work out perfectly. Instead, she continues to glide on, slightly shifting gears if need be. As long as she is doing what makes her soul happy, she trusts that she is living her best life.

FEARLESS & FABULOUS EXERCISE

What would your life look like if your inner muse were in control?

_____

_____

_____

_____

_____

_____

_____

Channeling your inner muse takes some work, but I'm going to clue you in on a few different ways you can accomplish it. First things first: you're going to have to drop your ego. Let go of all the bullshit (for a lack of a better term) and start tapping into yourself in a way you never have before. Let all the comparing go, let all of the worry go, and crawl inside the space in your heart that is so filled to the brim with passion and purpose that absolutely nothing on this planet can break it. I *know* you know what I'm talking about.

One way to accomplish this? Meditation. I know, I know, I threw you for a loop there. But stay with me for a moment. You're probably immediately picturing weird hippies waving incense around and chanting while banging on bongos. Believe me, I did too when I first started hearing about meditation. But it's not like that at all. I mean, maybe it is for some people, but not for us fabulous ladies (I'd never cramp your style like that). Meditation is a powerful tool that allows us to turn off our thoughts and tap into the deepest part of ourselves. Think about how many thoughts race through your mind from minute to minute. Our brains are on a constant loop and if we don't take time to clear all that chatter, we become overwhelmed and foggy. Aside from our own thoughts, we're also hearing everyone else. When is the last time you turned off the television and sat in complete silence? In meditation, we disrupt the unconscious progression of those racing thoughts and emotions by focusing on our breath, a mantra, or an image.

If you've never meditated before, start small. Even three-to-five minutes a day can have a powerful impact on your mind. You can either do a guided meditation, or listen to some soft sounds or music and do it on your own. Guided meditations are great, especially for beginners. Meditating on your own can also be wonderful as well. Here's a quick way to do a self-meditation: close your eyes and sit up straight with your feet planted firmly on the ground. Make sure your shoulders are back, and your chin is tucked under. As you breath in, envision the kind of life you want for yourself. Whatever that visual is, make it super clear. Maybe it's an image of you in a healthy, nourished body. Maybe it's an image of you running your empire in your office overlooking Central Park. Or perhaps it's a visual of you on a white sandy beach, with the waves crashing against the rocks. As you inhale, picture that image in your mind. As you exhale, breathe out all the negative thoughts and the things you do not want in your life; the anger, the fear, the frustration, the unhappiness. Picture them floating away as you release them.

And remember: whichever style of meditation you choose, allow yourself to find a quiet space, light some candles, and do everything you need to do to create a space of peace and tranquility. Channeling your inner muse should be your top priority, not something you squeeze in between a conference call and a diaper change. This is your Me Time. This is crucial to your well-being.

Meditation brings us to the here and now. It forces us to be in the present moment, letting go of all the stress we carry worrying about the past or the future. And as I've mentioned throughout this whole book, focusing on both of those things is often the root of our fear. When we get into the present moment, there is no space for us to experience worry or regret. Our only job is to experience exactly what is happening right now.

What I love most about meditation is that it allows us to connect with our natural state: a state of purity, peace, and happiness. You probably don't realize it, but that state is our default setting. You are meant to be happy all the time. Humans aren't meant to suffer and lead stress-filled lives. It's the outside forces of life that cloud us and make us feel frazzled, exhausted, and anxious. And it's those outside forces that breed our fear and stop us from leading the fabulous lives we're meant to live.

It may seem counterproductive to spend your time meditating after I've talked all about action. It took a long time for me to get into it. I am extremely Type-A, so you can imagine what slowing down felt like for me. I thought it was a total waste of time and I thought it would take me away from working on my business. But that could not be further from the truth. While action is extremely important in moving past fear and creating your future, slowing down and becoming centered is just as important, if not more. You have to meditate and connect with your inner muse at least once a day in order to unlock your most fearless and fabulous self. Trust me on that.

And I will not take excuses! I know you're busy. I know the kids are demanding little creatures. I know you're up to your ears in projects, and you still have to get to the supermarket and the dry cleaner. But if you are committing to everything I'm teaching you in this book, then you need to create some space for this daily practice. It will make you a better mother, wife, friend, daughter, employee, and an all around more fabulous person. Again, I'm not talking about thirty minutes. I'm not even talking about fifteen minutes. If you can devote even ten minutes a day to meditation, I promise you will see some pretty amazing results.

If you aren't a fan of meditation, or it's too difficult for you (believe me – I get it), then try exercise. A good old-fashioned sweat is a surefire way to clear your mind and release all of the stress and worry. In fact, I workout more than I meditate, but that's okay because working out *is* my meditation. There is something so empowering about walking into the gym and knowing that for the next hour or so, it's all about getting in my zone. I bring all of the stress and crap that I've accumulated that day and let it all go. I sweat it out, spin it out, run it out – whatever my choice of exercise is that day. I don't look at my phone other than to cue up my playlist.

You can channel your inner muse in whatever way works for you – just get there. Clear away all the bullshit from the outside world and find your girl. She's waiting for you.

FEARLESS & FABULOUS EXERCISE

Set aside at least twenty minutes per day to either meditate or workout in order to connect with your inner muse. Write down how you feel before and after.

_____

_____

_____

_____

_____

_____

_____

&FEARLESS
&FABULOUS

My inner muse is my natural state. I connect with this place by clearing my head.

YOUR FEARLESS AND FABULOUS LIFE AWAITS!

So here we are! In my typical *Champagne Diet* style, I'd suggest pouring a glass of bubbly (or sparkling water in a fancy glass) as we toast the end to this *fabulous* journey. You can go ahead and get one, I'll wait!

Let's review our manifestos. I'm a big fan of quick bites of positivity to inspire you on a moment's notice, so feel free to write these down and reference them whenever you need to.

FEARLESS & FABULOUS MANIFESTO #1
You can spend your energy getting excited or being afraid.
The choice is yours.

FEARLESS & FABULOUS MANIFESTO #2
You are forever changed as a person when you remain chained
to a life that is not aligned with your authentic self.

FEARLESS & FABULOUS MANIFESTO #3
Genuine confidence comes from within. Celebrate what you

love about yourself and give up your self-limiting beliefs.

FEARLESS & FABULOUS MANIFESTO #4
Nothing fabulous happens inside of a comfort zone.

FEARLESS & FABULOUS MANIFESTO #5
It's impossible to be afraid when you have an unwavering faith that everything will work out exactly as it should. Cultivate this faith every single day.

FEALRESS & FABULOUS MANIFESTO #6
The past does not define me. Every day is a fresh start to be the "haute couture" designer of my new and fabulous reality.

FEARLESS & FABULOUS MANIFESTO #7
By embracing fear, I take away its power over me.

FEARLESS & FABULOUS MANIFESTO #8
Fear would not exist if failure didn't. Redefine your definition of failure and look for opportunities to stretch and grow.

FEARLESS & FABULOUS MANIFESTO #9
I view my life as an adventure. The more I detach from the outcome of things, the more power I take back.

FEARLESS & FABULOUS MANIFESTO #10
My inner muse is my natural state. I connect with this place by clearing my head.

I want you to know how immensely grateful I am that you chose me to be a part of your experience in becoming a more fearless and fabulous woman. I hope that the tools and strategies I've taught you help you live a life that inspires you.

I am so proud of you for investing the time and energy into yourself by reading this book. Please understand that this is all a process. This book is the first step, but certainly not the last. Be patient with yourself. This book should be used as a reference guide, so come back to it as often as you need.

And finally, know that something more powerful than either of us can imagine led you to this moment. Know that you are in this exact place in your life for a reason and that the Universe is working in your favor. You are primed for greatness, so let go of believing otherwise.

Cheers to your new fearless and fabulous life!

With love and gratitude,

Cara

ACKNOWLEDGEMENTS

I am honored by the generous contributions of the women who helped make this book special: Jonna Spilbor, Keryl Pesce, Lisa Czarina Michaud, Victoria James, Annette Callan, Debbie Vasquez, Kelly Barkhurst, and Rachelle Walker. Thank you for being brave enough to share your stories. You are all an inspiration!

I am immensley grateful to Cara Loper at Loose Lid Creative, who has worked tirelessly with me for years on bringing these books to life. You are talented, dedicated, and patient. Thank you for everything, always.

To all of my readers, thank you so much for your support. I am so very thankful for every comment, email, tweet, and kind word. I appreciate each and every one of you more than you probably know.

To my husband, Ryan, for your endless support, kindness, and love. You have believed in me from the start and you make me feel like I can do anything. I love you!

ABOUT CARA

Cara Alwill Leyba is an Author and Master Life Coach from New York City. She is the founder of the popular blog, TheChampagneDiet.com, which has been featured in *Glamour*, *Shape*, *Cosmopolitan* South Africa, *Marie Claire* UK, *Daily Mail* UK, and many other sites and publications worldwide. Cara's writing has appeared in *The Huffington Post*, *Marie Claire* UK, MTV News, and others.

Cara runs an international boutique coaching practice where she works with women who are ready to make their happiness and priority. Through loving guidance, support, and an expert perspective, Cara empowers women to be the change agent in their lives. To learn more about Cara or to work with her, please visit www.CaraAlwill.com.

Connect with Cara:
www.Facebook.com/TheChampagneDiet
www.Twitter.com/ChampagneDiet
www.Instagram.com/TheChampagneDiet

Surprise! There's more!

Feel free to use the next few pages as your
Fearless & Fabulous diary. Write down anything that makes you
feel amazing: quotes, notes, ideas, thoughts, mantras...go crazy!

FEARLESS & FABULOUS

FEARLESS
&FABULOUS

FEARLESS
&FABULOUS

FEARLESS
&FABULOUS

CPSIA information can be obtained
at www.ICGtesting.com
Printed in the USA
FSOW02n0307200317
31724FS